Space Science

Written by Ciaran Murtagh

Contents

Look closely	2	Forces in space	12
Why experiment in space?	4	Being weightless	14
		3D printing	16
The International Space Station	6	Seeds in space	18
		The future	20
Sleeping in space	8	Glossary and Index	21
Different experiments	10	Experiments in space	22

Collins

Look closely

The International Space Station is a large spacecraft where astronauts can live. It circles Earth 15 times a day and travels around 350 kilometres above our heads. If you look closely, you can see it from Earth.

Right now, astronauts on the International Space Station are **conducting** experiments.

Why experiment in space?

Scientists working on the International Space Station want to discover information about the universe. Their experiments can last a long time because they live there for months.

These discoveries will help astronauts go on missions that will take them further from Earth.

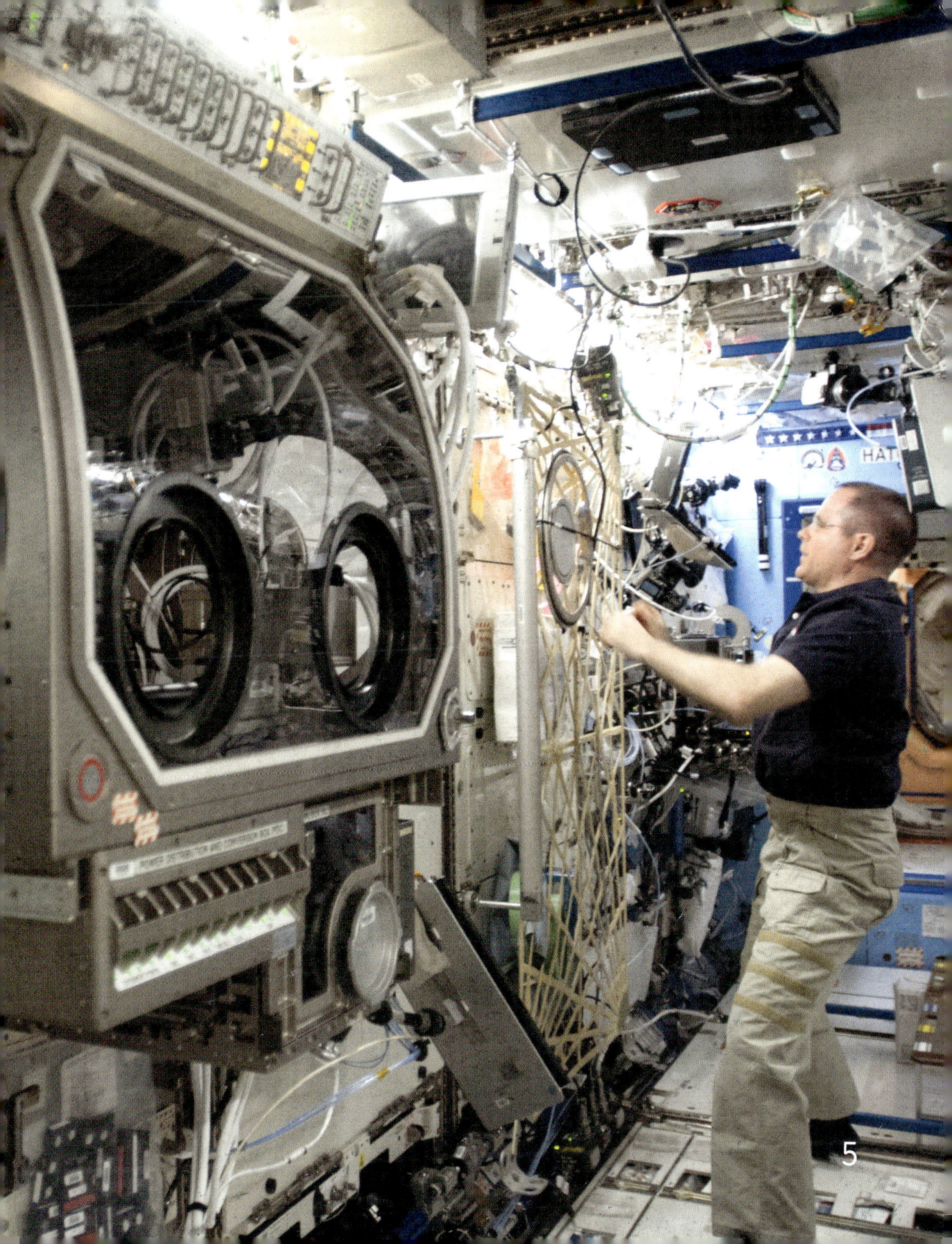

The International Space Station

Crews typically stay on board for about six months. They work from Monday to Friday and for half a day on Saturday. As well as conducting experiments, they have to keep themselves fit, eat and find time to relax and sleep.

7

Sleeping in space

On the Space station, there are 16 sunsets and sunrises every day so it's hard to know when it's time to go to sleep. Astronauts make sure they wake and sleep at the same time every day. Their cabin windows are covered to make it dark.

9

Different experiments

Experiments are conducted with plants, animals, humans, technology and technical equipment on the International Space Station.

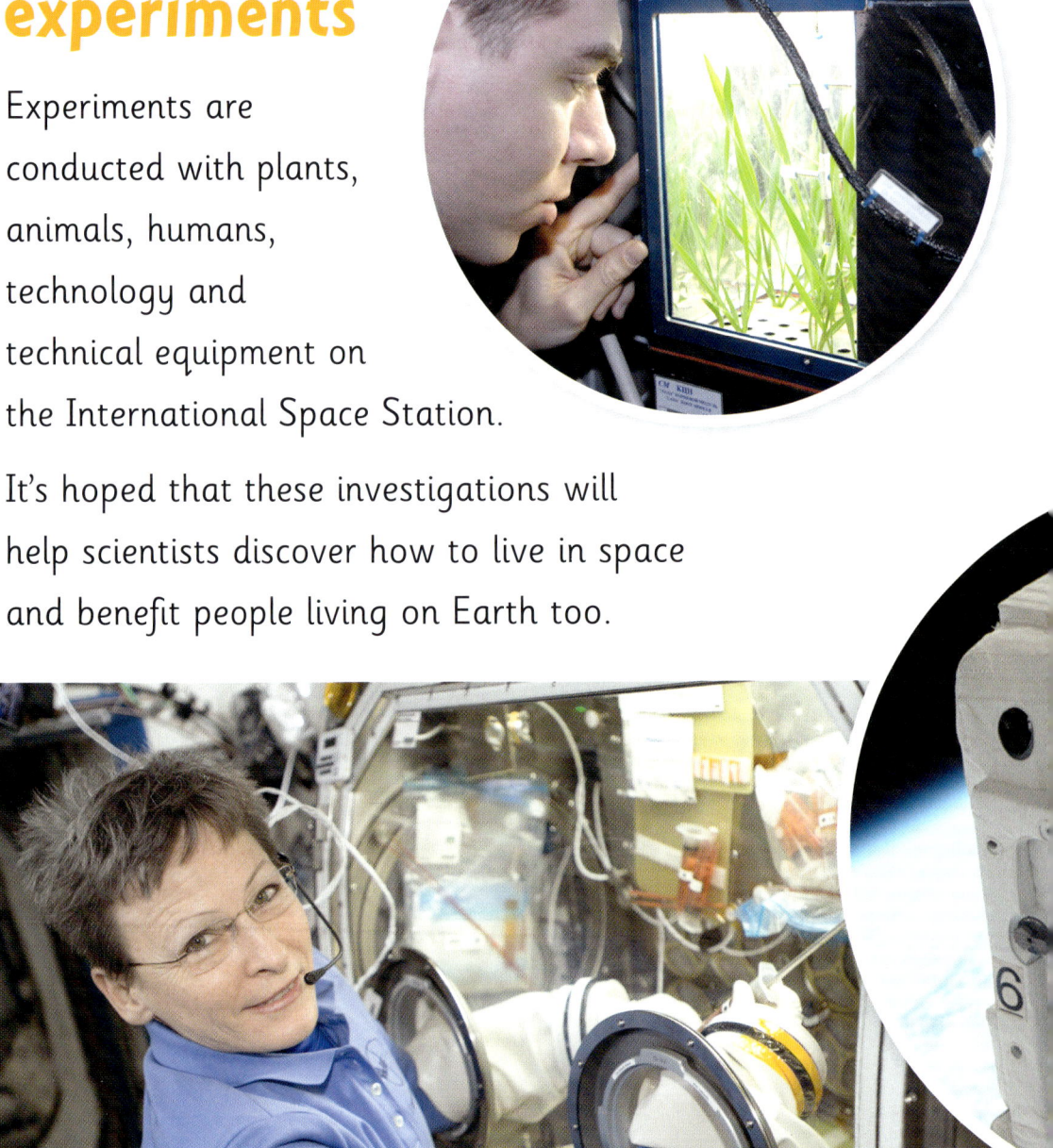

It's hoped that these investigations will help scientists discover how to live in space and benefit people living on Earth too.

11

Forces in space

On Earth, a force called gravity stops people and objects from floating away. In **orbit**, the pull of gravity is weaker, which is why things in space seem to be weightless. This force is called microgravity.

On the International Space Station, scientists use microgravity to learn things they would never know if they carried out the same investigations on Earth.

Being weightless

Many experiments conducted on the Space station focus on the astronauts. Scientists need to know what effects weightlessness will have on their bodies. This research will help them find ways to keep humans fit and well on longer space missions.

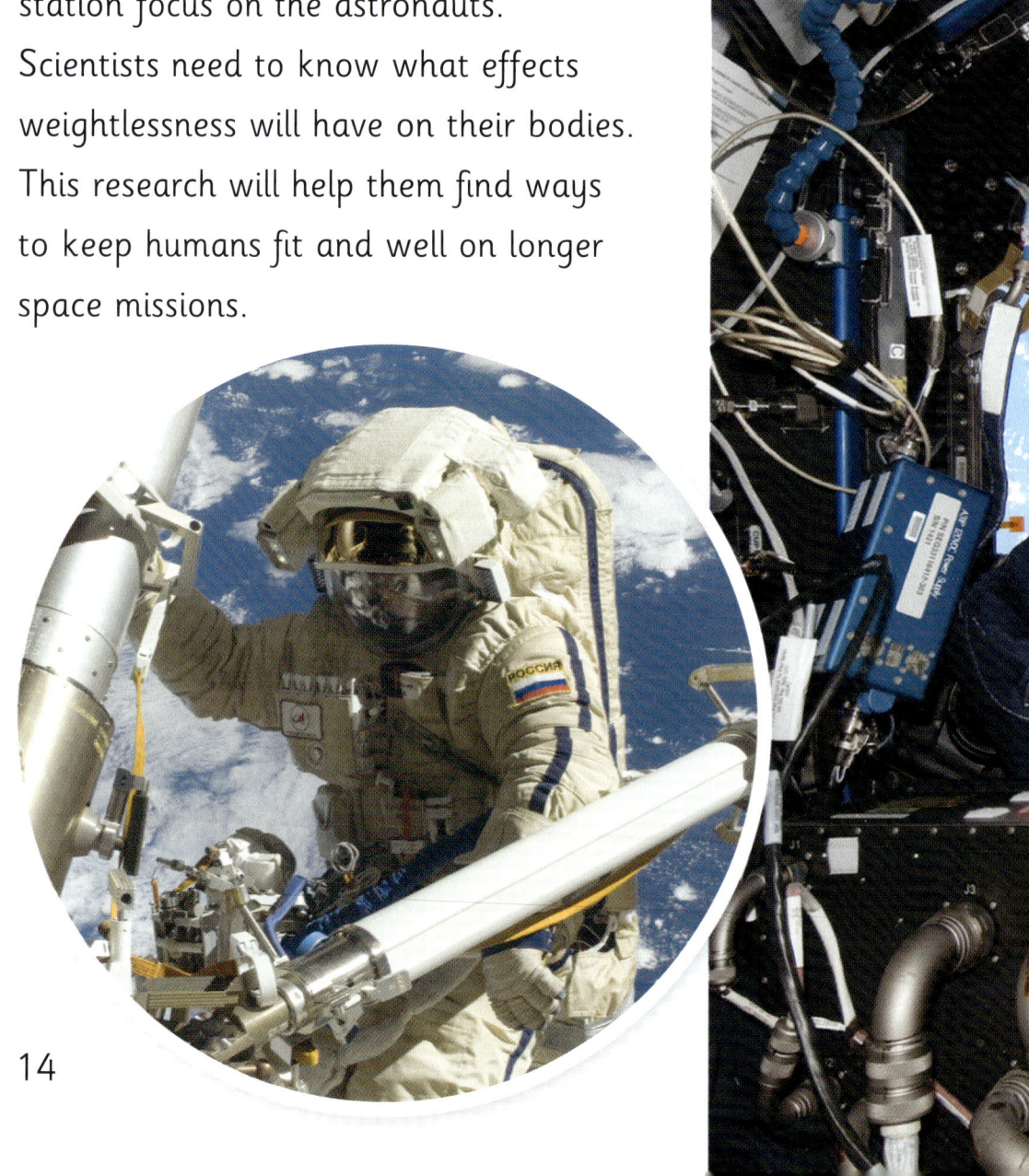

15

3D printing

A 3D printer prints objects instead of ink on paper. Scientists have successfully demonstrated that these printers would still work in microgravity. This means that, if a part breaks on a mission, astronauts could simply print a new one to fix it!

17

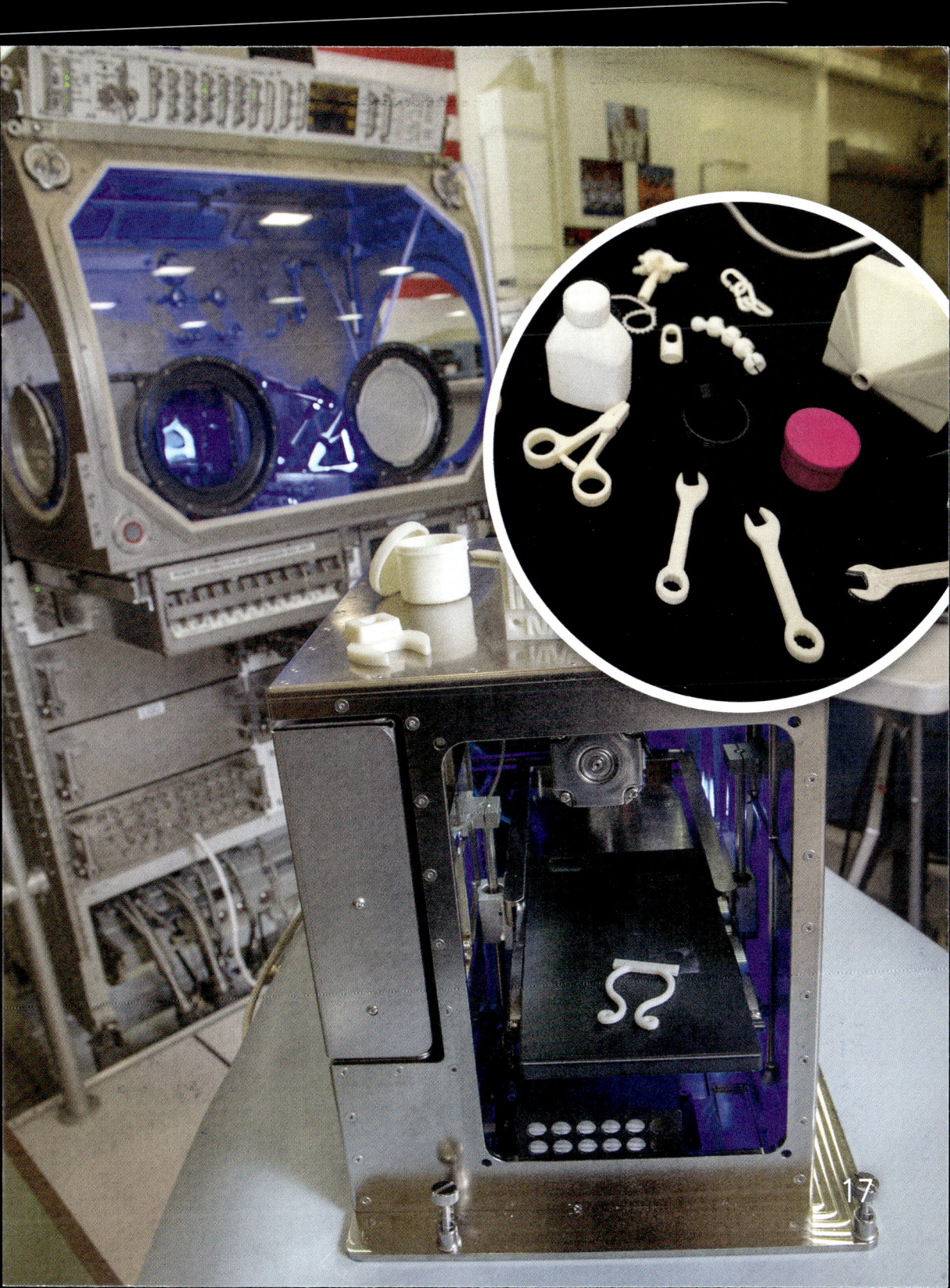

Seeds in space

Astronaut Tim Peake asked British schoolchildren to compare the growth of **rocket** seeds which had been in orbit on the International Space Station with ones which had not.

Over 320,000 measurements were collected making it one of the most detailed experiments ever carried out. This experiment demonstrated that seeds from space grew just as well back on Earth as seeds that hadn't been in orbit. Scientists now know they can take rocket seeds into space to grow their own food.

The future

Thanks to experiments conducted on the International Space Station, scientists know a lot about living in space. It's hoped that this knowledge will one day help astronauts safely travel further into space and even live there permanently.

Glossary

conducting   carrying out

crews   people who live and work together

orbit   a curved path in space that goes around Earth

rocket   a type of salad leaf

Index

astronauts 2, 4, 8, 14, 16, 18, 20

experiments 2, 4, 6, 10, 14, 19, 20

food 19

gravity 12

International Space Station 2, 4, 6, 10, 13, 18, 20

microgravity 12, 13, 16

Peake, Tim 18

sleep 6, 8

weightlessness 14

Experiments in space